ICELAND

NATURE, NURTURE & ADVENTURE

Diary of a Traveling Black Woman: A Guide to International Travel

Mini Travel Guide Series

Dubai, Abu Dhabi & The 5 Other Emirates You Didn't Know About

Jamaica: Likkle, but Tallawah!

Studying Abroad for Black Women

Teaching Abroad: From Abu Dhabi to Abuja

Solo Travel: Try It At Least Once!

and more...

Diary of a Traveling Black Woman:
A Guide to International Travel

"Mini Travel Guide Series"
Volume VI - Iceland
2nd Edition

Iceland:
Nature, Nurture & Adventure

Danielle Desir Corbett

The Traveling Black Women Network
Grace Royal International, LLC
Atlanta, GA

The intent of the author is to offer general information on visiting Iceland. The author assumes no responsibility for the actions of the reader.

Cover Model: Danielle Desir
Cover Design: Nadine C. Duncan
Interior Design: Nadine C. Duncan

ISBN: 979-8-9889182-8-8
ISBN: 979-8-9889182-9-5 (eBook)

2nd Edition, August 2023
Travel Guide Series, Volume VI

Published in the United States by:
The Traveling Black Women Network
Grace Royal International, LLC
Atlanta, GA 30316

www.travelingblackwomen.com

To Adventure.

CONTENTS

"My skin is melanated
&
My hair is curly."

PREFACE

After three trips to Iceland, this book shares the travel advice that I give my family, friends, readers of my blog - *The Thought Card*, and listeners of my podcast - *The Thought Card Podcast*. However, what sets this book apart is that it is intended to inform Black women how to plan an affordable, adventurous, and culturally enriching trip to Iceland.

Of course anyone can pick up this book and get value from the travel advice that I share, but the truth is that I am a Traveling Black Woman and as a Black woman, my experiences abroad may be different than most.

- As a Black woman, I am often traveling to lands far and wide where no one looks like me.

- My skin is melanated and my hair is curly.

- I usually don't speak the local language.

- I am constantly fighting stereotypes by educating others that Black people are way more than what is depicted in the media.

This book is not intended to exclude or polarize. In fact, it's meant to do the exact opposite. I want this book to inform and inspire more people to visit Iceland. Not only do I want people of color to travel more, I want to reshape the way people think about adventure. Iceland is much more than a destination. Iceland is an adventure.

Going on an adventure doesn't have to mean heading out into the wilderness, jumping out of a plane or doing something daring. It means extending yourself, broadening your horizon and being open to trying new things--all of which I have done in Iceland. Travel brings you face-to-face with the unusual and Iceland has a way of pushing you outside of your comfort zone.

This book is written by and for the traveling Black woman who is curious and eager to experience Iceland's incredible landscapes, unique foods, rich culture and strong sense of tradition. I wrote this book because I know that Black people, and black women in particular, face a lot of challenges while traveling such as facing fears, being ignored or objectified, not feeling welcome, being subjected to archaic stereotypes, being stared at or being told that we look like a black celebrity.

For the record, I look nothing like Serena Williams.

Although some things may be outside of our control, ladies, don't let any of these things hold you back from seeing the world. Don't let the possibility of a negative interaction abroad, limit you from the places you can visit. I certainly do not.

Another reason why I wrote this book is because I noticed the lack of current information about planning a trip to Iceland in print. When I first started to research, I went to my local public library in Bridgeport, Connecticut and there weren't any books on Iceland in the 'Adults Nonfiction' section. I had to go to the 'Juvenile Nonfiction' section where I found three books on Iceland with the most recent one dating back to 2006.

This got me thinking. How on Earth are Black people, and people in general, supposed to find out information about Iceland if their public libraries don't even have any information on it?

Tourism in Iceland is booming and I get that the internet, TV shows like Game of Thrones, movies, and social media play a big factor in spreading the word about it. But if local libraries, the central hub for books and other free resources, do not even have information about Iceland accessible to patrons, how will people who aren't online discover all that Iceland has to offer?

This bothered me and I wanted to change that. This motivated me to share my Iceland travel perspectives beyond the digital spheres of my blog and podcast.

If you're reading this, I'm excited that you are thinking about going to Iceland, and I'm here to tell you to do your research, plan your trip, and go!

BLOG POST ENTRY: MAY 9, 2016...

Hæ Hæ!! *(Pronounced hi-hi in English)*

"If you have been reading my blogs or following me on social media, you may have noticed that I have been obsessing over Iceland.

Iceland has been the #1 travel destination on my travel wish list and it's surreal to be here walking the streets, talking to locals and eating traditional Icelandic cuisine.

Even though I am jet lagged and have been running on sheer willpower, I wanted to quickly share some of the awesome things that have happened to me so far.

From the airport I managed to stay awake during the bus ride into Reykjavík and I'm so glad I did.

Driving from Keflavík International Airport to the capital, I wondered if I was still on Earth. Surrounded by rugged black and green lava rock, I felt like I was on another planet.

Off in the distance I could see the ice-capped Mount Esja and the glistening Atlantic Ocean to my right. From the little I've seen so far, Iceland's natural landscape is spectacular!

Within the hour I dropped off my things at Loft Hostel and walked in the general direction of the free city walking tour which started at 10 a.m.

I figured a walking tour would be a great introduction to a city and country which I know little about.

Knowing that my time on the island is short, can you blame me for trying to cram in as many things as possible?"

***

After visiting 26 countries and 3 continents, it's fair to say that Iceland is undoubtedly one of my favorite places in the world. Yes, that's right, in the world.

So far I've visited Iceland three times and I often find myself yearning to go back even if it's for a short weekend getaway.

Why am I so fond of Iceland?

If I had to sum it up into three words Iceland encompasses: nature, nurture and adventure.

I appreciate Iceland because although I've had my fair share of unique travel experiences in Iceland, I feel like I barely scratched the surface. I honestly don't think that Iceland will ever be a 'been there, done that' place for me, which is why I go back almost every year.

NATURE

From countless waterfalls to explosive geysers, colorful highlands and black sand beaches, Iceland has some of the most stunning panoramic natural landscapes I have ever seen. Even the simplest things like a rainbow over the bay will leave you in awe.

Iceland is also home to a lot of unique wildlife both on land and in the sea. On land, you can spot colorful puffins overhead, short and stocky Icelandic horses and the cunning Arctic foxes. You can also see seals off the coast and go whale watching.

Reykjavík, the nation's capital, is small compared to other European cities but it is colorful and charming. You can actually see the sky and there's only one building that towers above the rest. This makes it really easy to navigate. If you love coffee shops like I do, you'll be happy to know that there is a coffee shop on almost every street.

NURTURE

There's comfort in familiarity. As a black female solo traveler, I've found Reykjavík to be an approachable and walkable city. I felt safe exploring Reykjavík on my own (even at night). After visiting a few times you get to know your way around.

Icelanders are friendly and eager to share with

you their customs and way of life. They are also curious to learn more about you - where you're from, what you enjoy and how you see the world. Talking to an Icelander feels like a two way conversation. During my second solo trip to Iceland, I quickly became friends with a local. We still keep in touch years later and we've since traveled together to Ireland. We even met up in New York City last year.

ADVENTURE

Iceland offers travelers endless opportunities to explore, and I love that there is something new and exciting around every corner.

From touching a glacier tongue to snorkeling between the shifting North American and Eurasian tectonic plates, with each trip I'm bound to have an experience unlike any other.

As an adventurous traveler who is down for almost anything, except for bungee jumping, Iceland is my go-to travel destination for adventure and connecting with nature.

Where else can you hike into an ancient lava cave and later enjoy a hot pot bath out in the countryside?

In this travel guide I share my take on the island and all the essential things I think you should know before you go. I hope you find this information helpful and fall head over heels in love with Iceland as much as I have.

WHAT TO KNOW

"THE LAND OF FIRE AND ICE"

Nicknamed "The Land of Fire and Ice," Iceland is an island located in the North Atlantic Ocean halfway between North America and mainland Europe. It is the most western country in Europe and its capital Reykjavík is the northernmost capital in the world.

Iceland is home to some of largest glaciers in Europe and there are over 130 active volcanoes scattered throughout the island. Due to the volcanic activity, Iceland has a number of bubbling hot springs. Icelanders harness their energy from the underground geothermal heat to inexpensively heat their homes and pools.

VIKING ORIGINS

Iceland has an interesting origin story. Although sailors knew it existed as early as the fourth-century, the island was first settled by Nordic Vikings. Vikings were known to raid and trade along the coast of the North Sea.

Iceland has a rich storytelling culture and according to Landnáma (The Book of Settlements), an ancient medieval text, Ingólfur Arnarson is said to be the first permanent Norse settler around 874 A.D. Historians acknowledge that Irish monks and hermits lived on the island before the Norsemen, but they decided to leave since they did not want to live with pagans.

Exiled from Norway because of a blood feud, Ingólfur Arnarson set out with his family and Celtic slaves and settled in what he called "Reykjavík" or "Smoky Bay." The name Smoky Bay is only befitting of an area where steam rises from nearby hot springs. You can find a statue of Ingólfur Arnarson in downtown Reykjavík on top of Arnarhóll Hill.

WHERE DO MOST ICELANDERS LIVE?

Most Icelanders live in the greater Reykjavík area. Reykjavík is the capital of Iceland and its largest city. More than likely, this where you will call 'home' during your trip.

Akureyri is the second largest city in Iceland and it is located north of the island. Nicknamed the Capital of the North, Akureyri is a major fishing harbor (which does not freeze in the winter) and the center of tourism for the northern region of the country. Akureyri is a 5 hour drive from Reykjavík via The Ring Road but you can take a bus, hop on a flight (takes approximately 30 minutes) or get there by boat.

TRIP PREPARATION

To make the most of your trip to Iceland, here is what you need to know before you go to Iceland including airport information, visa requirements and more...

FLYING TO ICELAND

Icelandair is an Icelandic airline that offers daily flights from North America and Europe to Iceland throughout the year. You can also fly with other popular airlines like Delta, United Airlines, American Airlines, Air Canada and more, however, it's important to note that some routes are seasonal.

When you fly across the Atlantic via Icelandair, you can add a stopover in Iceland at no additional cost for up to 7 nights. This offers travelers an affordable way to experience Iceland without having to spend extra money on airfare.

Although this may fluctuate, according to Inspired by Iceland, over 25 airlines offer flights to Iceland.

AIRPORT INFORMATION

Keflavík International Airport (KEF) is Iceland's only international airport and it is the hub for national carriers like Icelandair. Most travelers visiting Iceland will land at this airport.

Keflavík International Airport should not be mistaken with Reykjavík Airport which only offers domestic flights within Iceland. Keflavík International Airport is modern and compact. It has one terminal named after Leifur Eriksson, the first European to arrive in North America (long before Christopher Columbus).

The first floor features a check-in area and services like VAT tax refunds, customs, currency exchange and banking and bus ticketing. The second floor has lots of tax-free shops, cafes, restaurants, bars and terminal gates. Wi-Fi at the airport is unlimited and free. There are also a lot of ATMs at the airport.

While walking in the airport, be on the lookout for interesting art exhibits. 'Directions' by Steinunn Þórarinsdóttir is actually one of my favorites. You can find it right outside of the arrivals hall. The aluminum sculpture features four people looking in opposite directions. Also, if you're into comic books, Keflavík International Airport has a large colorful hand painted ceramic tile mural which should not be missed.

Keflavík International Airport is approximately 40 minutes or 28 miles from Reykjavík and a 20-minute drive from the Blue Lagoon, one of the most popular attractions in the country.

Fun Fact: The Keflavík International Airport was built by the U.S. military during World War II, however since 2006, the airport has been used solely by civilians.

ENTRY REQUIREMENTS

All visitors require a valid passport to visit. Since Iceland is part of the Schengen Agreement, U.S. citizens and Canadian citizens can enter Iceland for tourist or business purposes without a visa for up to 90 days in a six-month period.

For U.S. citizens, a three-month passport validity is required after your trip, but it's recommended that your passport be valid for at least six months after you travel. You also need two blank pages in your passport to meet the entry requirements.

For the full list of countries whose citizens need a visa, visit the Icelandic Directorate of Immigration website for the latest visa information.

Helpful Tip: Before booking your flight to Iceland, visit your embassy's website or contact your embassy to confirm visa requirements. If you need a visa to travel to Iceland, get it early or at least do your research to know the requirements.

VACCINATIONS

No vaccinations are required for traveling to Iceland. During the winter, flu shots may come in handy. However, you should check your embassy's website for the most up to date information.

PACKING

Since Iceland's weather is unpredictable. Regardless of when you plan to visit, plan to wear layers and bring warm, windproof, and waterproof clothing with you. Unlike other places where what you pack is determined by the time of year, this is not necessarily the case in Iceland. Always dress in layers.

Wind and rain are common regardless of the time of year you visit. Iceland is known to have sunshine, high winds, snow and rain all on the same day.

Regardless of what season you visit, here's what you should add to your Iceland packing list:

	This guide
	Passport
	Photocopy of passport
	Driver's license
	Poncho, raincoat or waterproof jacket (with a hood)
	Flashlight (if driving)
	Headlamp light
	Fast drying towel
	Backpack

	Flip-flops
	Reusable water bottle
	Thermos
	Camera, tripod, batteries, and lenses
	Extra memory card
	Rechargeable batteries
	Universal or European power adapter
	Portable charger(s)
	Sunscreen
	Swimsuit
	Sunglasses
	Hair products
	Sleep mask
	Medicine/prescriptions (as needed)
	First Aid kit
	GPS
	Journal
	Reusable bags
	Microspikes (optional)

Wardrobe Packing List

	Hat, ear muffs, scarf, and gloves
	Wool socks
	Sweater
	Thermal long sleeves
	Layering tees
	Heavy coat
	Waterproof boots
	Waterproof pants
	Hiking shoes (with good grip)
	Leggings
	Jeans
	Waterproof/hiking pants

Avoid wearing cotton or jeans while exploring the outdoors. Cotton holds onto moisture and you'll feel colder faster when it's windy.

Bring your own hair products with you to Iceland. Hair products for kinky and curly hair may be hard to find.

Helpful Tip: Since it rains sideways in Iceland, umbrellas aren't useful. Locals never use umbrellas, so bring a poncho or waterproof raincoat with a hood instead.

POWER ADAPTER

There are two major power outlet differences between the U.S. and Canada, and Iceland. First the outlets are shaped differently and second, the power voltage is different. Iceland uses North European electrical standards (50 hz/220 volts) and the standard European two round prongs. The U.S. and Canada have a standard voltage of 110 volts (or 60 hz) and use two flat prongs. With that being said, if you're coming from North America, you will need to use either an adapter or converter to charge your electronics.

WHEN TO USE AN ADAPTER VS. A CONVERTER?

North American travelers will need either a converter or adapter because Iceland's outlets have a higher voltage. To charge devices like your cell phone, camera or laptop, all you need is an adapter to change the shape of the power plug to fit into the shape of Iceland's outlets. Most devices are "dual voltage" which means that they work in both North America and Europe.

However, if you are bringing small appliances, changing the shape of the plug with an adapter might not be enough so in that case you'll need a converter. A converter is more complex because it converts one input power into a different output power. Adapters are relatively cheap while converters are generally more expensive. (For example, bringing a hair dryer from North America to Iceland will require a converter and is not recommended.)

Helpful Tip: If you forget to pack your converter or adapter, converters and adapters are available at duty-free stores in the airport, supermarkets, bookstores, souvenir shops, and hotels.

WHAT TO EXPECT

PROS & CONS FOR BLACK WOMEN

As it relates to Black women, here are the benefits of traveling to Iceland as a Black female traveler...

GREAT DESTINATION FOR SOLO TRAVEL

If you've never done a solo trip before, Iceland is a great place to start. Two out of my three trips to Iceland were solo.

- Iceland is very safe. Most people speak English, and it's not too far from the U.S. or Canada. In fact, Reykjavík is only 5 hours (via airplane) from the east coast of North America.

- Connectivity is also strong in Iceland and it is easy to navigate.

- The locals are warm and welcoming and there are a ton of things to do from partying in Reykjavík to hiking the mountainous terrain, exploring inside volcanoes and glacier climbing to name a few.

- If you enjoy the outdoors and nature, Iceland is a remarkable destination.

- As a solo traveler, I recommend booking bus tours.

Guided bus tours provide transportation, a guide and sometimes admission to certain attractions or national parks. I've found that this is the most affordable way to get around and sightsee hassle-free.

FRIENDLY LOCALS

With over 335,000 people populating the country, I appreciate Iceland because it isn't very populated and the nation's capital has a small-town vibe.

Everyone seems to know each other and locals are friendly and will engage in conversation with you. They are often curious to know what you think of their beautiful country so be prepared to share your answer.

EASY TO MEET PEOPLE

One of my favorite things about Iceland is that there are a lot of female solo travelers visiting Iceland so it's easy to meet other people when you join bus tours and stay at hostels. During two of my solo trips to Iceland I befriended other female solo travelers from the U.S., New Zealand and Singapore. We still keep in touch via social media.

Every year I see more and more Black people traveling to Iceland. It's always nice to see other Black people traveling the world. Give them a head nod, smile or wave.

EASY TO JOIN GROUP TOURS

Another benefit to Iceland is that there are a lot of tour operators. As a female solo traveler you can easily join a group tour even the night before in some instances. Alternatively you can easily rent a car and explore on your own.

Personally, I enjoy group tours because they help me navigate unfamiliar territories in the comfort of a group so that I'm not alone.

ENGLISH IS WIDELY SPOKEN

Do Icelanders speak English?
Yes, they do!

Although, the official language in Iceland is Icelandic. English is widely spoken in Iceland. English is taught as a second language in school as well as other languages like Danish (Denmark), Swedish (Sweden), German, Spanish or French. Most Icelanders speak more than one language and almost all Icelanders speak English, however people over 50 years old may not speak English fluently.

CONS FOR BLACK WOMEN IN ICELAND

I will lead with this: The Iceland tourism board states, "Iceland is not for everyone. It's not for those who go where everyone else goes. It's not for the conservative and expected traveler."

I wholeheartedly agree. Iceland will expand your horizon and may challenge you. If you don't like the cold weather, Iceland may not be for you. If you aren't an adventurous traveler and if you are not open to trying new things and experiencing different cultures, then Iceland may not be the right travel destination for you.

Another con to traveling to Iceland as a Black woman is that you will stand out. For a long time, Icelanders were a homogeneous population with similar ethnic makeup. That makes Black folks and people from other ethnicities the extreme minority.

As you travel around the country, you will see very few people of color in Iceland. Historically, immigration to Iceland was limited, however, some people of color do live in Iceland. This is especially true if you venture off into the countryside or other remote areas. However, that should not stop you from visiting Iceland.

Locals may stare at you, but it is usually not out of hatred or disrespect. It is usually out of curiosity. Personally, I've found that if I find people staring at me while I'm abroad, they usually...

> 1) ...haven't seen many Black people before
> 2) ...are curious why I'm visiting
> 3) ...are admiring my beauty.

When people stare at you and make you feel uncomfortable, they might not realize what they're doing. You can break up the awkwardness with a smile, wink or a wave. I try not to pay too much attention or get offended when people stare at me because I understand that it usually is unintentional. If this happens to you in Iceland, remember that Icelanders do not grow up in a diverse culture.

I personally have not had any confrontations with racism in Iceland. I also haven't experienced any cat calling in Iceland either.

SAFETY

As a Black woman traveling throughout Iceland, I felt safe walking around in Reykjavík as well as traveling throughout the country (I've visited various places around the country via bus tours). The crime rate in Iceland is extremely low and violent crime is virtually non-existent. Also, if it's any consolation, the majority of police (over 95%) are unarmed in Iceland.

According to the Iceland 2018 Crime and

Safety Report, The U.S. Department of State assessed Reykjavík as a low-threat location for crime. Crime in Iceland is lower than most developed countries or countries of similar size. According to the report, the high-standard of living, small population and social attitudes toward crime all contribute to the low crime rate in Iceland. Despite this, I still advise using precaution. Keep your valuables close and remain alert.

There was only one time where I felt uncomfortable as a Black woman in Iceland:

> A few years ago I was walking from my hostel to Hallgrímskirkja Church, approximately a 9-minute walk. I was walking on Laugavegur, one of the main shopping streets in downtown Reykjavík when I felt like I was being followed. A young man was walking ahead of me and kept looking back at me. He did this often enough where I started to feel uncomfortable. I quickly realized what was going on so I called my mom, got her on the phone and ducked into a side street. He stopped following me after that. Honestly, my gut tells me that I caught his attention because I was a Black woman...

As with anywhere you travel to, it's important to remain alert and be aware of your surroundings at all times. As you know, you will stick out in Iceland so it's important to take immediate action when you feel uncomfortable.

In rural areas, the biggest threat to your safety will likely be nature or weather conditions. With that being said, response times to emergencies may be slower out in the countryside.

***

Helpful Tips:

- Always keep your phone charged - bring a power bank with you. Your phone is an important life line to navigate and stay connected with your family and friends back home.

- 112 is the emergency number for police, fire and ambulance in Iceland. All operators speak English. Have this number on speed dial during your trip.

- For medical or non-emergencies dial 544-4114 during business hours. Outside of normal business hours, dial 1770. A nurse will offer advice, suggest a clinic, or send a physician to make a house call.

CLIMATE

Due to strong oceanic currents, Iceland's climate is mild. The average temperature in January (the coldest month) is 32°F or 0°C. July which is considered the hottest month of the year has an average temperature of 52°F or 11°C.

The best time to explore Iceland depends on what you want to see and do during your trip. Regardless of the time of year you visit, make sure you wear layers because the weather changes suddenly. It's better to have too much clothing on than not enough.

SPRING

Spring in Iceland is short. It falls between April and May. There are usually fewer tourists visiting Iceland and only a slight chance that you may catch the Northern Lights. Unlike other places around the world, you might be surprised to find out that Iceland may be dreary during this time of year.

Spring is when the snow starts to melt, flowers start to bloom and the days get longer. During my last spring trip to Iceland, it was still light outside around 10 p.m.

SUMMER

From June to August expect long, bright days. The peak of Iceland's midnight sun is June 21st. During the summer months, the sun hardly sets. This is called the "Midnight Sun." Expect endless daylight throughout the day and night. Be sure to bring a mask to help you sleep. Most accommodations have blackout curtains as well.

During the summer, Iceland's landscape is lush green. You can enjoy outdoor activities like hiking, cycling, horseback riding, bird watching, camping and going to festivals. The summer is also perfect for road tripping around the country since roads to the highlands start opening up.

Summer Pros:
- Midnight sun (longer daylight hours)
- Longer exploration times
- Plenty of outdoor activities
- Access to interior roads and the highlands
- Animal migration (whales and puffins)
- Wild sheep roaming the countryside

Summer Cons:
- Peak tourist season
- Tours, food and car rentals are more expensive
- May have a hard time finding accommodations

- May have trouble sleeping at night due to the constant daylight
- Not as warm as you might expect for summer weather
- Can't experience the Northern Lights

FALL

Fall is similar to springtime. The leaves and moss are changing colors and it's likely rainy, windy and snowy. Although it's hard to predict, usually autumn in Iceland is between August and October. Days are typically getting shorter and it's easier to see the Northern Lights around this time.

WINTER

If you plan on traveling to Iceland during the winter months then be prepared to brace yourself for the frigid climate. Winter is between October and March. Expect lots of windstorms, snow and ice. Car rentals tend to be cheaper during the winter months.

One of the benefits to the short daylight means that you can gaze at the picturesque Northern Lights for hours on end. The shortest day of the year falls on December 21st, the winter solstice. In Reykjavík that typically means only 4 hours of sunlight.

I prefer visiting Iceland during the off-season

since flight prices are usually cheaper. I've traveled there both in the spring and fall and I loved it. Yet, many recommend visiting Iceland in the summer and winter to experience the contrast.

Winter Pros:
- Northern Lights
- Snowy landscapes
- Frozen waterfalls
- Hearty soups and stews
- Christmas and New Year festivities
- Cheaper for tourists
- Ice caves and glacier walks

Winter Cons:
- Darkness for much of the day
- Shorter exploration times
- Most unpredictable season
- Frequent road closures and no access to the highlands

Weather is one of the important things to keep in mind when planning a trip to Iceland. Weather conditions vary. Regardless of what season you visit, expect rain and strong winds during your trip. The winds in Iceland are intense.

Since the weather can change within a blink of an eye, listen to the local weather forecast 24-48 hours in advance for the best predictions. Icelanders usually use the Icelandic Meteorological Office called Veðursto-fa Íslands to check out the expected weather conditions.

TIME ZONES

Iceland is on the Greenwich Mean Time (GMT) all year round. That means that it does not observe Daylight Savings Time. Depending on the time of year (winter or summer), Iceland is between 4 or 5 hours ahead of the East Coast of North America.

CURRENCY: ICELANDIC KRÓNA (ISK)

Helpful Tip: Download a currency converter app to easily track currency exchange rates.

The Euro, US Dollar and Canadian Dollar are not accepted in Iceland. Although cash is accepted everywhere, Icelanders usually pay for everything with either a credit or debit card. Mastercard and Visa are widely accepted. However, you might run into issues trying to use American Express.

In Iceland, currency exchange rates are usually the same at banks and tourist information centers so there's no need to shop around There are ATMs throughout Reykjavík and there is a bank inside Keflavík International Airport.

PRACTICAL $$ TIPS

From glacier hiking to trying new foods or relaxing at local swimming pools and hot tubs, there are plenty of interesting things to see and do in Iceland. Yet it won't be long until you notice that Iceland is an expensive travel destination.

How expensive is Iceland?

According to Numbeo's 2019 Cost of Living Index, it is the second most expensive country in the world. Since most goods are imported, the cost of living is high. This includes things like gas, food, alcohol and clothing. Iceland is a very expensive country and it might not be the best destination for frugal travelers. Despite this, don't assume that you can't visit on a budget. There are a lot of ways to save money on your trip. With a little creativity, some research and planning, you can manage your expenses and make your travel savings stretch further. Remember, nature is abundant and free here. That means go out and explore waterfalls, rivers and natural hot springs for free.

Here are some of my favorite practical tips for saving money in Iceland:

- *Plan a Shorter Trip*

  While spending a few weeks in Iceland may sound appealing, if you don't have the funds to go on a long trip, that doesn't mean that you should cancel your trip completely. If you're on a budget, plan to spend fewer days in Iceland. You can do a lot in 3-4 days.

- *Visit Off Season*

  Traveling off season means that you can find better deals and save money across the board. September to November and March to May will likely be less crowded.

- *Shop Duty Free*

  Why is alcohol so expensive in Iceland? Alcohol is expensive because it is heavily taxed. Alcohol taxes are levied based on the alcohol content per drink so the more alcohol per volume, the more expensive it will be.

  For those financially savvy travelers who want to enjoy a drink in Iceland, my first piece of advice is to buy alcohol duty-free at the airport. Assuming that you're flying into Keflavík International Airport, be sure to stop by Duty-Free Iceland. It is a one-stop shop that offers lower prices on domestic and international liquor (along with other items). Before you go on an alcohol spending spree, keep in mind that by law, each traveler is only permitted six units of alcohol. Sounds confusing? Use an alcohol-allowance calculator to see how much alcohol you can buy at the airport: "Iceland Duty Free Allowance Calculator."

APPY HOUR

My second piece of advice is to make the most of local happy hour specials in Reykjavík by downloading the Appy Hour app. This free app sorts out all the bars and restaurants offering happy hour specials based on proximity and price.

AVOID BOTTLES OF WATER

There is no need to buy bottled water. All Icelanders drink from the tap (faucet). You can get free water anywhere, even fresh streams, under a waterfall or at a glacier. Yes, I drank water from a glacier lagoon and it was delicious. Give it a try!

Not only is Iceland's tap water drinkable, but it is also never chemically purified. It is said to originate from springs. The water is naturally purified by molten rocks which not only cleans the water of any bacteria or chemicals but also adds essential minerals and nutrients.

Bottled water is the same as the water that comes from the tap so don't waste your money on it. Also by refilling your water bottle, you're preserving the environment.

Helpful Tip: If the hot water in Iceland smells like sulfur, don't be alarmed, just let it run for a bit.

CLAIM YOUR TAX FREE REFUND

Make sure to claim your tax refunds before leaving Iceland. Tax free shopping is a great way to save money, but since the claiming process is rather involved, let me walk you through it.

What Is Tax Free Shopping?

Tax free shopping is when you buy goods in a foreign country and get a refund for a portion of the sales tax. Refundable sales tax has all sorts of names like goods and services tax (GST), value added tax (VAT) or consumption tax. In Iceland, it's called tax free shopping. It is another way to save money especially when you're traveling to an expensive country.

Tax free shopping in Iceland applies to goods that are purchased there for 6,000 ISK or more. In other words, the original receipt must show at least 6,000 ISK spent, this can include sales tax. It also doesn't matter how many items you buy to reach the minimum spend. As long as they are on the same receipt, you are good to go.

Only visitors or non-residents are eligible for tax free shopping in Iceland and you can only claim up to 14%. Restaurants, hotels and tour activities do not qualify.

Other Iceland Tax Free Shopping Restrictions:
- You have to exit the country with your goods and claim the refund within 3 months of purchasing
- Foreigners with permanent residence in Iceland are not entitled to refunds
- You have to have the items with you during departure

When you're shopping, after you make a qualifying purchase, ask the store clerk to fill out a tax free form. To claim your refund, the original receipt must be signed by the vendor and it has to be attached to the tax free form.

When I bought a raincoat in Iceland, the tax free form was conveniently located below the total on the receipt. The vendor stamped my receipt and handed me an information packet that not only included a guide to help me get the most out of tax free shopping but it also had a pouch where I stored my receipt (and Iceland tax free form). The information section was in English but also translated into German, Russian and Chinese.

Overall the form was easy to complete. I included my name, address, country of origin, credit card number (the credit card I used to buy the goods), passport number and signature.

As a recap, when it comes to tax free shopping in Iceland, here's a summary that breaks down who does what:

1. *Retailer Fills Out*
   - Retailer signature/or stamp
2. *You Fill Out*
   - Full name
   - Address
   - Country
   - Passport number
   - Customer signature
   - Credit card number
3. *Customs Fills Out*
   - Stamp with date and signature

HOW TO GET VAT REFUNDS IN ICELAND

Keflavík International Airport

Before checking in and passing through security, follow the "Tax Refund" signs. In case you need help locating the kiosk, your Iceland tax free information packet has a map that you can follow.

Why Claim Refunds Before Checking-in?

It's important to claim your Iceland tax free refund before checking in because customs may ask to see your purchase(s). They may also ask for your passport and boarding pass. Also, once you clear security, you will not be able to claim your refund again. And just in case you're wondering, you can't mail your forms in later.

In my case, the customs officer did not ask to see my raincoat. She checked that all the information on the form was complete and stamped my receipt. She then asked if I'd like my refund in cash or credited back to my credit card. I chose the latter since this was the free option. If you choose cash, you'll have to pay a service fee. This all took a few seconds. Remember, if your receipt doesn't have a stamp or signature from the vendor, you will not be eligible for a refund.

Other Departure Points

If you aren't flying out of Keflavík International Airport, you can still claim your tax free refund aboard sailboats, cruise ships, and private planes. In these cases, the customs officers will come onboard before departure.

How Long Does It Take To Get Your Iceland Tax Refund?

After you submit the form, it takes anywhere from six to eight weeks for you to get your refund. I received mine eight weeks later.

TIPPING CULTURE

Tipping isn't mandatory in Iceland. No need to tip your waitstaff, taxi drivers, bartenders, porters at hotels or tour guides. In fact, Icelanders don't tip at all because service is already included in the bill. The price you see on the menu is the total amount including tax and service.

If you feel like your server or bartender went above and beyond, feel free to tip but there's no obligation or expectation. You may also see tip jars in coffee shops. But remember: you don't have to tip unless you want to. In Iceland, people earn reasonable wages and do not rely on tips to get by.

GROCERIES

When looking for reasonably priced items to stock your fridge, visit Iceland's budget grocery stores Bónus and Krónan. Bónus is easy to spot around Reykjavík (yellow with bright pink pig logo). Both Bónus and Krónan are among the most well-known and reasonably priced in Iceland, with a large assortment of household items like snacks, drinks, fresh produce and just about anything else you might need to comfortably enjoy your stay.

Avoid 10-11, the most expensive grocery store in Iceland. Also stay away from the 24/7 shops because they tend to hike up the prices.

Helpful Tip: Grocery store hours vary so go early and avoid waiting until the last minute because some grocery stores close early on the weekends or they might not even be open on Sundays.

To save even more money, avoid going out to eat as much and cook your own meals instead. Breakfast and lunch are generally easier to cook. Most guesthouses and hostels have kitchens that you can use no questions asked. Many travelers also bring their own food and stock up on perishables when they get to Iceland.

I suggest planning to go out to eat a couple of times so you don't miss out on trying authentic Icelandic foods. Avoid buying food at gas stations if you are on a budget. You can also bring your own coffee and tea from home to save money at the cafes.

DON'T HAGGLE

Icelanders don't haggle and they think it's rude to try to negotiate the price. The only place where haggling is generally accepted is at flea markets like Kolaportið.

STAY CONNECTED

Staying connected is easy. Coverage is generally reliable, however you may find that your signal gets weaker in remote areas. The country area code is +354. To place a call in Iceland, dial 354 and the seven-digit number. To place an international call to Iceland dial 00 plus the country code and seven digit number.

Generally Wi-Fi is accessible and free of charge. Many establishments including cafes, hotels, bars, libraries, book stores and even some gas stations offer free Wi-Fi.

Helpful Tip: If you're from the U.S., some service providers offer unlimited international texting and internet in Iceland for free; no roaming charges. If your phone is unlocked, you can also purchase a Vodafone SIM Card with a data plan and local number.

CULTURAL NORMS

One of the great things about traveling to new countries is immersing yourself in the local culture. Not only is Iceland's population small in size but they pride themselves in being a close-knit society with a strong sense of cultural identity and family values. Understanding the local culture helps to not only give you context but when you are interacting with locals, you will better understand where they are coming from.

RESPECT THE ENVIRONMENT

Icelanders are very respectful of the environment and travelers should follow suit. That means do not litter, pick up trash when you see it, and pack a reusable water bottle. Icelandic people also try to stay on beaten paths and they encourage visitors to do the same. Do not step on the moss and always leave nature as you found it.

ICELANDIC LAST NAMES

Unlike other Western cultures, Icelandic family members follow Old Norse tradition and they do not have the same family last names (surnames). Women generally do not change their last names when they get married.

Icelandic last names are taken from their father's (sometimes mother's) first name and add either a 'son' if it is a boy or 'dóttir' if it is a girl. Your father's first name + son or dóttir = Your last name.

For example, a man named Eric has a son named Jonas. Jonas would be Jonas Ericson, meaning son of Eric. In most cases Icelanders' last names indicate the father and not the family lineage. That means that Icelanders only share the same last name with their siblings of the same sex, not their siblings of the opposite sex, parents or grandparents.

Icelanders also call each other by their first names so plan to do the same. Even if you are addressing a doctor, lawyer, teacher or politician.

LOVE AND MARRIAGE

Icelanders are family oriented, however, marriage isn't a big deal. Most couples are not married and most children are born to unwed parents.

A HAPPY COUNTRY

Despite the Viking's raiding past, today Iceland is considered one of the world's happiest countries. According to the World Happiness Index, in 2019, it ranked #4 right behind Norway (#3), Denmark (#2) and Finland (#1).

LANGUAGE

Icelandic is the official language spoken in Iceland. Since the population is small, Icelandic is spoken by very few people which makes it a vulnerable language. Many say that it is a difficult language to learn, understand and speak. The present day Icelandic language traces back to Old Norse (Norwegian) with North Germanic roots. Since the first Norse (Norway) and Celtic (Irish) settlers in the 9th century, Icelandic hasn't changed much.

As a small island isolated from mainland Europe, while the Old Norse language spoken across the Nordic countries has evolved, Icelandic has stayed virtually the same. Icelanders can still read ancient Icelandic Sagas from the 10th and 11th-century. Today Norwegian and Icelandic are two different languages.

Icelanders are passionate about protecting and maintaining their language, and cultural identity. November 16th is 'Icelandic Language Day' which celebrates the preservation, protection and advancement of the Icelandic language. You might also find it interesting that Icelanders don't have regional dialects. Icelandic is pretty much the same everywhere you go.

Common Icelandic Words and Phrases
- Hi - Halló
- Thank You - Takk
- Yes - Já
- No - Nei

TRANSPORTATION

Keflavík International Airport (KEF) is approximately 45 minutes away from downtown Reykjavík by car. To save both time and money, it's best to plan how you will get to/from the airport ahead of time. There are several transportation options available.

AIRPORT EXPRESS BUSES

The most convenient way to get to Reykjavík from the airport is to take an airport express bus. There are two main airport express buses in Reykjavík: FlyBus Airport Shuttle and Gray Line Iceland Airport Express. Taking a bus is a great option if you don't feel like driving. Although you can order bus tickets at the airport counter, I recommend booking online to save time and money.

Departures are scheduled 25-45 minutes after arriving flights so even if you arrive late at night or early morning, there's always a bus available. The ride takes approximately 45 minutes, Wi-Fi is free onboard and the seats are comfortable.

Both Gray Line and FlyBus can drop you off at the BSÍ bus terminal (the main bus terminal in Reykjavík) or for a little extra, you can get dropped off near your accommodation. If you opt for the latter, you'll have to transfer to a mini bus. Since vehicles holding more than eight passengers or more are banned in downtown Reykjavík, the mini bus will drop you off at the nearest stop and you'll have to walk a few minutes to your accommodation.

Since the Blue Lagoon is only 15-20 minutes from the airport, many travelers opt to visit it either on arrival or departure. FlyBus and Gray Line can take you to the Blue Lagoon, back to the airport or downtown Reykjavík. Both companies also offer popular day trip excursions like Golden Circle Tours or tours to the South Coast of Iceland.

Helpful Tip: Before booking your airport shuttle, Google "Gray Line promo codes" or "FlyBus promo codes" to find coupon codes for more savings!

*This information was previously published online at thoughtcard.com.

RENTING A CAR

Renting a car is a popular option for travelers visiting Iceland, however it is pricey. Fuel is not cheap and neither is the rental fee, especially if you are traveling solo. The price of the rental depends on the season, the length of the trip and the type of vehicle.

Due to Iceland's extreme weather conditions, the additional car insurance for gravel protection, sand, ash and ice is highly recommended. However, you can skip the theft protection since car theft is virtually non-existent in Iceland.

Outside of the capital, gas stations may be few and far between so keep a close eye on your gas meter and fill up wherever possible. Do not let your gas level fall below half tank!

There are lots of car rental companies with the majority based in Reykjavík and Keflavík International Airport (KEF). Picking up your rental at KEF and dropping it off before your return flight is the most convenient option. If you are from North America, driving in Iceland will feel familiar because you drive on the right side of the road.

To rent a car in Iceland all you need is your passport, credit card and a valid driver's license. No international driver's license is needed.

In Iceland, manual rental cars are usually cheaper than automatic cars. Having the right vehicle for the time of year you're visiting and what you're planning to do on your trip is very important. During the summer months rent a 2WD vehicle and in the winter rent a 4WD vehicle. 4WD vehicles are more expensive but allows you to access more rugged places.

If you are renting a car in Iceland, consider staying outside of Reykjavík because you won't need to drive inside the city center.

Helpful Tip: The most affordable rentals tend to sell out quickly, so book as early as possible. The earlier you book, the more options you will have. Expect higher prices when you book last minute.

DRIVING IN ICELAND

The Ring Road encompasses the entire island and has two lanes (one in each direction). You can see lots of popular attractions on The Ring Road like Skógafoss and the Jökulsárlón glacier lagoon. The general speed limit is 50 km/h in urban areas and 90 km/h on paved roads.

In the winter, plan ahead for possible delays. Icy road conditions are common and since the roads are narrow, this can be very dangerous. Outside of the city there are few traffic lights and lots of roundabouts and single lane bridges. All passengers are required to wear seat belts.

Although it might be tempting, do not go off the road. Not only is it dangerous but you can seriously damage the vegetation and natural environment which may take nature years to repair. Off-roading is strictly forbidden in Iceland, you will get fined if you do. Follow the signs and if a road is closed, do not go there.

For visibility, always carry a flashlight and keep your vehicle's headlights on. Icelandic law requires vehicle headlights to be on during the day and at night.

If you want to take a photo of the natural scen-

ery while driving, stop at a nearby parking area and walk back if you have to. Stopping your car in the middle of the road is very dangerous and can lead to an unnecessary accident.

Icelandic lamb and sheep outnumber the human population by roughly 2:1 so be on the lookout for these roaming white 'land clouds' while driving around. If a car hits a livestock, the driver is expected to be held liable for any losses. So if you do see any sheep nearby, it's best to slow down and pay attention. They tend to run out on the road unexpectedly.

And, it goes without saying... do not litter.

RENTING A CAR VS. JOINING A BUS TOUR

First and foremost, there is no right or wrong way to explore Iceland. It all comes down to personal preference, time and travel style. When traveling solo, I prefer bus tours because they are easy to book and more affordable than renting a car. However, when traveling with family and friends consider renting a car. You can split the bill and save money across the board on the rental, fuel and insurance.

Although there are many things that may influence your decision to either rent a car or join a bus tour, if you need help figuring out which option is right for you, consider: affordability, convenience and flexibility.

AFFORDABILITY

Bus tours are a cost effective way to explore Iceland especially if you are traveling solo. Not only do you avoid having to pay for car rentals, the cost of fuel, collision insurance, gravel protection, ash and ice insurance, navigation and metered parking, but many bus tours include a local guide and admission to paid attractions.

For example, my Snaefellsnes Peninsula day trip included hotel pick-up and drop-off service, round-trip transportation, a professional tour guide and a guided lava caving tour of the impressive 8,000-year old Vatnshellir Cave (valued at 3750 ISK or $38 USD). From Reykjavík, this 11-hour bus tour took us through small fishing villages in West Iceland, coastal shorelines, black-pebbled beaches, iconic landmarks like Kirkjufell Mountain and mossy lava fields.

I've found that bus tours can offer incredible value at a competitive price. Although there are many Iceland travel agencies that offer guided day tours, some companies may sweeten the deal by offering special discounts during off-peak season. Others may combine multiple attractions and offer discounted combo tours. Besides bringing money for souvenirs, snacks and lunch (optional), on bus tours, everything is usually included. All you have to do is show up, have fun and be mindful of departure times.

HASSLE FREE

For travelers looking for a less involved, hassle-free travel experience, a bus tour may be the better option when sightseeing. You don't have to do your homework ahead of time. No figuring out which types of cars to rent or worrying about running out of gas. You also don't have to worry about horses, sheep or even reindeer in the middle of the road (which seem to be a frequent occurrence in Iceland when it is warm out).

On a bus tour, you can fall asleep in the comfort of your seat, strike up a conversation with a seatmate or access the web via complimentary Wi-Fi onboard while your driver navigates the roads. You also avoid speeding fines from speed traps.

Last but not least, it's important to consider the weather. How comfortable would you feel driving in Iceland's notoriously unpredictable weather conditions? During my recent trip to Iceland, my tour group got caught in an Icelandic winter storm. The wind gusts were so high that the waterfalls in the South Coast of Iceland were flowing in the opposite direction, an amazing natural phenomenon! However, there were times when I thought that the wind would blow our minivan off the road, so I knew that I would not have felt comfortable driving on my own.

If you intend to rent a car during the winter, ask yourself, am I experienced enough to deal with Iceland's winter driving conditions? As a rule of thumb, if you're not comfortable with driving in strong winds, ice and snow, keep calm and join a bus tour.

FLEXIBILITY

When it comes to flexibility, renting a car is the best option because you can drive at your own pace, stop and take photos, create the perfect itinerary that matches your interests and visit as many attractions as you like.

With a car, you can take detours (safety first though) and make frequent photo stops without reservation or time constraints. Spend more time at the attractions that resonate with you and skip the rest. This is not possible with bus tours. Bus tours have a set itinerary, specific driving route, set bathroom breaks and pit stops. In a nutshell, bus tours are on a strict schedule and they operate outside of your control. This means that there's little to no flexibility.

Although some bus tours offer optional activities during a stop (like free walking tours), at the end of the day, a stop is a stop. Worse case scenario, if you miss a departure, your bus can potentially leave you behind which I bet is extremely stressful. If you're looking for flexibility, renting a car may be the better option.

Both renting a car and joining a bus tour in Iceland has its pros and cons. Many people prefer day tours because you have access to an expert guide at all times and you can ditch the responsibilities of driving. On the other hand, many travelers who rent cars value the freedom that comes with venturing off the beaten path and appreciate not having time constraints even if that means that they won't have access to a local guide. Driving in Iceland doesn't have to be burdensome, but it is important to be prepared.

Regardless of which sightseeing route you choose, I'm confident that Iceland will blow you away.

PUBLIC TRANSPORTATION

Iceland's public bus service, Strætó operates in metropolitan Reykjavík while Strætisvagnar Akureyrar services Akureyri. Outside of the capital, public transportation is limited. From Keflavík International Airport you can take Bus 55 to Reykjavík city center. Although taking Bus 55 is the cheapest option, you should take into account the limited schedule especially on weekends.

Bus tickets can be bought at supermarkets, shopping centers, public libraries, swimming pools and bus terminals, or you can use the Strætó app (available on both Apple and Android devices). If you decide to pay on board, bring exact change with you because bus drivers do not carry change. To get from one major city to another Icelanders usually take a domestic flight.

Fun Fact: There are no trains in Iceland.

TAXIS

Although taxis are convenient, they are the most expensive option for getting to/from the airport and around Iceland. Taxis run by the meter and accept all major credit cards. At Keflavík International Airport (KEF) you can find them right outside the airport terminal. Depending on where you are staying, you can expect to pay over $200 USD from KEF to the city center.

Taxis in Iceland don't have a uniform design or branding as do yellow cabs in New York City. They vary in make and model, but all cabs have a yellow taxi sign on the roof. Taxis can be booked by phone or at taxi stands throughout downtown Reykjavík. Hreyfill Bæjarleiðir and BSR are the most popular companies used for hailing a cab around Reykjavík. Uber, Lyft or other ride sharing apps are not available in Iceland.

Besides catching a cab, renting a car or taking public transportation, there are still lots of other ways to get around. You can explore by boat, plane, bike or ATV.

ACCOMMODATIONS

There are all sorts of accommodation options in Iceland. Prices vary but hostels, guest houses, Airbnb rentals, hotels and camping are all available options. The earlier you make your reservation, the more likely it is that you'll find a reasonable priced option, so book your accommodation as soon as possible. Do your research. I do not recommend winging it, be sure to plan ahead.

Helpful Tips:

- If you are staying at a hotel that offers breakfast at an additional cost, skip it. You can find cheaper options on your own by either going to a cafe or going to a grocery store.

- Booking an Airbnb or guest house with a kitchen that allows you to cook your own meals is ideal. It will save you a lot of money on food.

TRADITIONAL ICELANDIC FOODS

Traditional Icelandic foods include lamb, dairy, bread, potatoes and seafood, however don't be surprised if you come across other types of meats like horse, reindeer and puffin. Stew and soup are also popular in Iceland. It's also important to note that when Icelanders eat 'lamb', they eat everything on the lamb including its testicles!

How adventurous do you want to get with trying Icelandic foods? From most adventurous to least, here's a list of some of the most popular Icelandic foods to try:

FERMENTED SHARK

Hákarl (or fermented shark) is traditionally cured Icelandic shark. Back in the day, the curing or "fermentation" process included burying the shark underground for 3 months and later hanging it to dry for four to five months. This gets rid of the acidity and makes it edible.

The smell alone may be enough to keep you away but if you're brave and want to give it a try, you can find fermented shark at fish shops, flea markets and at supermarkets. You can also find fermented herring and skate (fish). Rinse it down with a shot of Brennivín or "Black Death," an Icelandic schnapps. Avoid touching the fermented shark to prevent the lingering smell on your skin.

What does fermented shark taste like? Hey, I'm adventurous, but I'm not *that* adventurous!! Many say that fermented shark has an ammonia taste to it so no fermented shark for me!

SOUR RAM'S TESTICLES

Sour ram's testicles are washed, boiled and served pickled. They are usually sliced down and look similar to a slice of bread. It's most common to find sour ram's testicles in the winter during the Þorrablót winter feasts. You can also wash it down with a shot of Brennivín.

SVIÐ

Sheep's head anyone? Smoked sheep head is one of the unique foods that you can try while visiting Iceland. The entire head is eaten and the cheek, tongue and eyes are said to be the best parts.

SLÁTUR

Slátur is traditional Icelandic blood pudding which is eaten by a lot of Icelanders. This dish is made out of sheep guts, blood and fat.

HARÐFISKUR

Harðfiskur (or stockfish) is dried fish that you can find in any grocery store or at fish shops. Harðfiskur is usually dried naturally with the wind and it can be eaten as a snack. Many locals eat it with butter.

HANGIKJÖT

Hangikjöt is a traditional Icelandic smoked lamb commonly served with potatoes, creamy sauce, and canned peas. It's also a popular lunch food eaten with butter on top of "Flatkaka", Icelandic rye bread. You can find this in pretty much every supermarket.

PYLSUR

Served on a warm bun, pylsur (or hot dog) is made from Icelandic lamb, beef, and pork. Add toppings and sauces like raw or fried onions, ketchup or mustard. You can buy a hot dog at any gas station in Iceland. In downtown Reykjavík, order a hot dog from the legendary Bæjarins Beztu Pylsur, the famous hot dog stand close to the harbour. Unfortunately for the non-meat eaters, they do not offer vegan hot dogs. Pylsur is the only real Icelandic "street food" you'll find around.

RYE BREAD

Icelandic rye bread is very popular and absolutely delicious. It's dark and slightly sweet. Eat it with butter or accompany it with smoked lamb.

Right across the street from Hallgrimskirkja Church, dine at Cafe Loki for homemade rye bread and traditional Icelandic food. Rye bread and herring was my favorite Icelandic dish. I recommend giving it a try!

SKYR

If you haven't had a chance to try Skyr. I highly recommend it. Pronounced "skee-er", it is a dairy product that resembles yogurt but it has a milder taste. Although it's technically classified as a cheese, most people mistakenly call it yogurt. Skyr is one of Iceland's oldest dairy products and has been around for nearly a thousand years. Instead of having a sour, tart taste, the cultures that make up skyr have a rich and creamy flavor. It is also very good for your health. It contains more protein and less sugar than yogurt.

In Iceland, you can find all sorts of skyr flavors like peach cloudberry, strawberry, banana, apple, raspberry, coconut and more. Trying skyr is one of the inexpensive things that I recommend doing in Iceland if you're on a budget. You can find Skyr at grocery stores, gas stations and even some restaurants.

Helpful Tip: Skyr served at restaurants or other major tourist attractions is usually more expensive than skyr found at grocery stores.

ICE CREAM

Icelanders love ice cream and they eat it all year round. While in Iceland, I highly recommend trying the ice cream, it is delicious.

If you're driving along the Golden Circle in Iceland, I recommend stopping by Efstidalur 2 for homemade ice cream. This family run farm has been around since 1850 and overtime it has grown to include horse rentals, a restaurant and a bed and breakfast. Although you can order salted caramel, white chocolate and licorice, strawberry and vanilla were my favorites. I especially liked that Efstidalur 2's ice cream is creamy and flavorful but not overwhelmingly sweet. Made with local ingredients, the milk is sourced fresh from the farm's cows. If you are a vegan, some ice cream shops serve soy or coconut based ice cream. After you've had your fill, go see some of the calves next door or admire the beautiful countryside views before hitting the road.

In addition to traditional Icelandic cuisine, the food and restaurant scene in Reykjavík has plenty of options from unique Icelandic foods, fine dining experiences, cheaper eats and international cuisines.

MY TOP FOOD PICKS

- Rye bread from Cafe Loki in downtown Reykjavík.
- Fish and chips at Icelandic Fish and Chips.
- Sweet rolls, bread, croissant and other baked goods, at Brauð & Co in downtown Reykjavík. There are several locations.
- Soft serve ice cream at Efstidalur 2.
- Coffee and Haitian food at Cafe Haiti.
- Vegan or vegetarian at Gló.

You can find many vegan restaurants as well as gluten-free or vegetarian-options on restaurant menus in Iceland. It's also easy to find other popular foods like pizza, burgers, and Asian cuisine.

At places that sell french fries, you'll also find a spe cial pink sauce in Iceland. For the most part, this pink sauce is a mixture of ketchup and mayo, among other things. Icelanders call it kokteilsósa or cocktail sauce and it is tasty! In Iceland you won't get regular mayo at most fast food joints.

WHAT TO DO

MAJOR ATTRACTIONS IN REYKJAVIK

You'll find that there is something for everyone. Here are the major attractions to visit in Reykjavík.

CITYWALK REYKJAVIK FREE WALKING TOUR

The free walking tour with CityWalk Reykjavik was one of the first things I did when I arrived in Reykjavík and I highly recommend it. This two-hour historic tour offers a great introduction to the capital city and Icelandic culture. The insightful CityWalk guides are Icelandic history graduates and high school teachers. The tour is fun and engaging.

During the tour, you will visit the most historic parts of downtown Reykjavík including Arnarhóll Hill and Fógetagarður Square. At the end of the tour, set your own price. Tip what you feel the tour is worth. The tour guides rely solely on the contributions from attendees. You can even tip in any currency you like which is convenient.

CityWalk also runs a pub crawl, a tour on the Icelandic economy and various private tours.

HALLGRIMSKIRKJA CHURCH

You can see the Hallgrimskirkja Church from

just about anywhere in the city. It's the tallest building in Reykjavík and it is said to be where you can get the best possible views over the oldest part of Reykjavík. Admission to the church is free, but to climb to the top of the tower and see 360-degree views of Reykjavík, the harbor, and Mount Esja, you will have to pay a fee. From the top of the church you will see that the city of Reykjavík is filled with colorful row houses. The houses are painted in bright pastel colors. They are made of concrete so they can stand up to natural disasters like earthquakes and strong coastal winds. Before making your way to the church, be sure to check the hours of operation.

WALK AROUND LAKE TJÖRNIN

This is one of most scenic places in Reykjavík! There are plenty of swans, geese and ducks to admire at Tjörnin, so bring your camera. When you're done, head over to the Reykjavík City Hall. On the main floor, there is an impressive 3D topographic map of Iceland.

SUN VOYAGER

Along the waterfront, visit the Sun Voyager which pays homage to the first Icelanders. Although it looks like a Viking ship, it's actually a dreamboat following the setting sun. As you enjoy the cool breeze, marvel at the rainbows and take in the gorgeous view of Mount

Esja alongside the iconic Icelandic landmark.

HARPA CONCERT HALL

Right on the Old Harbour, the Harpa Concert Hall is a modern concert hall and conference center with a 'distinctive colored glass facade' inspired by Iceland's basalt landscape. At night the glass changes color. Harpa is home to a variety of events, concerts and shows. You can visit the concert hall for free.

MUSEUMS

Here are a few museums in Reykjavík that you might want to check out:

- *The Saga Museum* - Step back in time, try on traditional Viking outfits, take photos and learn about Iceland's early history. The audio tour is included in the price of admission and it takes about 30 minutes to get through. This museum gears more towards kids.
- *The Settlement Exhibition* - This interactive museum focuses on the first settlers of Iceland and their lifestyles from 874 A.D. to 1262 A.D. It shares findings from archaeological excavations of Viking longhouses in the city center. It takes about an hour to get through.

- *The Icelandic Phallological Museum (The Penis Museum)* - This museum has more than 200 animal penises and penile parts on display. Getting an audio guide is recommended.

SHOPPING

If you enjoy shopping, you'll enjoy walking along Laugavegur (the oldest shopping street in Reykjavík), Bankastræti, Austurstræti and Skólavörðustígur streets. Here you can find small shops, high-end boutiques, restaurants and bars. Keep in mind that this is a touristy area so prices will be high. Other shopping options include visiting Kringlan and Smárilind malls. These are further away from the downtown area.

Kolaportið Flea Market is an indoor market where you can find the most affordable Icelandic wool sweaters, vintage wear, and food. This is the only place in Reykjavík where you can haggle. The market is only open on the weekends.

Helpful Tip: Not all Icelandic wool sweaters are created equal. If you are looking for authentic Icelandic wool sweaters be sure to buy from local farms, the Kolaportið Flea Market or the Hand Knitting Association of Iceland shop in downtown Reykjavík. There are lots of shops in Reykjavík that state their sweaters are "original Icelandic" only to find out that they were made in China.

LOCAL SWIMMING POOLS

Soaking in a hot thermal bath or taking a dip in a swimming pool is an important part of Icelandic culture. Not only do the geothermal (naturally heated) waters offer therapy but an outdoor soak is a recreational activity that many locals enjoy.

In Reykjavík there are 17 public swimming pools but nearly every town in Iceland has at least one. And although the luxurious Blue Lagoon is one of Iceland's most popular geothermal pools, there are many alternatives to check out.

HOT SPRINGS/ HOT POTS

Natural hot springs (hot pots) are sourced from geothermally heated groundwater. Some hot springs are extremely hot while others are perfect to bathe in. And while some hot springs in Iceland are easy to find, others may require a hike off the beaten path. Hot springs range from free to an entry fee which usually includes access to on-site changing rooms and showers.

THERMAL POOLS/SWIMMING POOLS

Icelanders love to soak in hot tubs and cold pools. Even if it's raining or snowing you will still find locals socializing and unwinding at these local pools. Swimming pools (sundlaugs) are open year round. They are often outdoors and heated with geothermal water. Although some lack the spa-like amenities, many feature hot tubs and cold tubs, water slides, wave pools, steam baths, jacuzzis and saunas.

While the Blue Lagoon is one of the most visited attractions in Iceland, it is rather expensive. An alternative to visiting the Blue Lagoon is to visit local swimming pools. You can find a swimming pool in nearly every town in Iceland. These swimming pools have hot tubs and cold tubs and they are significantly cheaper than visiting the Blue Lagoon.

- Laugardalur is the largest swimming facility in Reykjavík. It has an Olympic-size pool, several hot pots, a steam bath and more.
- Vesturbæjarlaug is less than half an hour walk from the city center. Vesturbæjarlaug is a traditional outdoor thermally heated swimming pool in a suburban neighborhood right outside of Reykjavík. Although it's smaller than the other popular swimming pools in town, it offers plenty including two outdoor pools, six hot tubs, one cold tub, two saunas and a steam room. I particularly enjoyed their hot tubs.

Lastly, don't forget that if you're on a budget, Iceland is abundant in nature which is free. Consider hiking, visiting national parks, black sand beaches or waterfalls without ever spending any Icelandic Króna.

STREET ART

While window shopping, be on the lookout for street art. You can find it all over Reykjavík, just look on the sides of the buildings. Each mural tells a story and makes a bold statement.

THINGS TO DO OUTDOORS

Most outdoor activities in Iceland are free. You can walk right up to them or it's a short hike away.

Looking to join a group tour or bus tour? There are all sorts of options to choose from. From small group tours that offer a personalized experience to large group tours, here are the most popular tours to join:

- Golden Circle Tours
- South Coast of Iceland
- Snaefellsnes Peninsula
- Whale Watching and Puffin Tours
- Snorkeling Silfra
- Horseback Riding
- Helicopter Tours
- Northern Lights
- Snowmobile Tours
- Game of Thrones Filming Locations
- Ice Cave Experience

BLUE LAGOON

Blue Lagoon is one of the most visited attractions in Iceland. It's warm milky waters are a big draw for tourists all over the world. Since the Blue Lagoon is so close to the airport, you can visit the Blue Lagoon on your way to Reykjavík or before departure.

The Blue Lagoon is touristy and quite expensive so book in advance to save time on the long lines. If you're on a budget and want to have a similar experience, consider the natural geothermal pools that you can visit in Iceland. Many

SOUTH COAST OF ICELAND

The South Coast of Iceland is one of the most visited regions in the country. Not only is it easy to get to and from Reykjavík but there is a variety of things to see and do. The South Coast of Iceland is home to glaciers, glacier lagoons, waterfalls, lava caves, black sand beaches and more. Enjoy activities like hiking, horseback riding, kayaking or glacier walking. Most of these experiences you'll have to do with an experienced guide.

SAMPLE ITINERARIES

Helpful Tip: When planning your Iceland itinerary, take both the weather and available daylight hours into account. For example the weather and the number of daylight hours in January and July are different. January has a lot less daylight hours and more icy road conditions than in the summer months.

SOUTH COAST OF ICELAND ITINERARY

SKÓGAFOSS

Skógafoss is a majestic 200 feet waterfall. It is one of the largest waterfalls in Iceland and a popular destination to visit on the South Coast. Skógafoss is so powerful that I could feel the spray even at a distance. Expect to get wet, so wear a waterproof jacket and boots to stay dry.

Aside from the sheer size, one of the striking things about Skógafoss is the surrounding greenery. Both the cliffs and the neighboring turf are lush and green.

On the side of the waterfall, there are stairs that lead to a lookout offering fantastic views as far as the Atlantic Ocean. The five hundred and twenty-seven steps lead to one of the most notable hiking and trekking trails on the island. There are over twenty waterfalls to see on this route, so technically, Skóga-foss is only the beginning.

THE SECRET GLJÚFRABÚI

Don't miss Gljúfrabúi, a secret waterfall hidden in a canyon. I have to say that I would have missed it completely if I wasn't on a guided tour. Since there is no footpath into the narrow gorge, hop from rock to rock until you reach inside the cave. Stepping in the river is inevitable, so I would recommend wearing a pair of sturdy waterproof boots.

Inside the canyon, the cascading water looks like it is pouring down from the heavens. The cave has no roof which allows for lots of sunlight to shine through. To the right, there is a large boulder called Franskanef (the French nose). Franskanef partly covers the base of the waterfall. Carefully stand on it for a different perspective.

SELJALANDSFOSS

From the secret Gljúfrabúi, walk across a lush green field to a waterfall, unlike the rest.

Seljalandsfoss is a testament to Iceland's breathtak-ing natural beauty and it is one of the only waterfalls that you can walk behind, weather permitting of course.

At the bottom of the cliff, walk up the footpath that loops behind the falls. Although the climb doesn't look intimidating, I would recommend taking it slow. The footpath is wet and slippery. Behind the waterfall, you can see the surrounding meadow and look down at the pool flowing into the Seljalandsá River.

After visiting Seljalandsfoss, warm up with a cup of coffee or hot chocolate inside the Seljalandsfoss Shop. The Seljalandsfoss Shop serves warm soup and freshly made sandwiches as well as souvenirs like knitted Icelandic sweaters and lava jewelry.

GOLDEN CIRCLE ITINERARY

The Golden Circle is one of the most popular routes to tour in Iceland. It loops from Reykjavík to the South Coast and back. Along the route you can visit the Geysir, Gullfoss Waterfall and Þingvellir National Park. Although this is one of the first things that most tourists do when they get to Iceland, I decided to go against the grain and only toured this area during my third trip to Iceland.

ÞINGVELLIR NATIONAL PARK

Þingvellir National Park is a UNESCO World Heritage Site. This is where the Althing - The Iceland General Assembly for Parliament (the world's first democratic parliament) was established in 930 A.D. This is also the only place in the world where you can walk or snorkel between the shifting North American and Eurasian tectonic plates.

GULLFOSS WATERFALL

Gullfoss (Golden Falls) is one of Iceland's most popular waterfalls. From several vantage points, explore the two tiers of this mighty cascading waterfall.

GEYSIR

Known as Strokkur or "The Great Geysir", this is the geysir which all of the other geysirs in Iceland are named after. Every 8-10 minutes or so, bubbling hot water erupts from the ground. Expect the smell of sulfur.

WATERFALLS TO VISIT IN ICELAND

- Goðafoss
- Seljalandsfoss

- Gullfoss
- Skógafoss

MY ICELAND TRAVEL WISH LIST:

- See Northern Lights
- Swim in the Blue Lagoon
- Drive Golden Circle
- Hike Mount Esja
- Glacier Lagoon
- Diamond Beach
- Go on an ice cave tour
- Jökulsárlón
- Experience midnight sun
- Solheimasandur Plane Wreck
- Secret Lagoon
- Myvatan Nature Baths

NIGHTLIFE

Icelanders like to party. Downtown Reykjavík is a lively place on Friday and Saturday nights. Since alcohol is pricey, most Icelanders pregame (or pre-party) ahead of time at home and they don't go out until midnight. That means if you want to check out Reykjavík's party scene, go out late and plan to be out until the wee hours of the morning. And yes, you can expect to hear your favorite American tunes in various bars and clubs.

ICELAND TRAVEL PLANNING RESOURCES:

I hope that you found this travel guide insightful! Now that our time together has come to an end, I know that there are a lot of things to consider when planning an epic trip to Iceland.

While there is still so much that I have yet to see and do, Iceland is an unforgettable adventure which I hope you get to experience for yourself sometime soon.

Here are a few resources for your convenience:

Iceland Emergency Numbers:
- Emergency Number: 112
- Police: 444-1000
- Medical Assistance: 1770

Icelandic Meteorological Office: Vedur.is (https://www. vedur.is/) - weather and aurora forecast in Iceland.

Road.is (http://www.road.is) - road condition updates in Iceland.

Hot Pot Iceland (https://hotpoticeland.com) - comprehensive list of hot springs and swimming pools in Iceland.

DIARY

_____

_____

_____

_____

_____

_____

_____

_____

_____

_____

_____

_____

_____

_____

_____

_____

_____

ABOUT THE AUTHOR

Danielle Desir Corbett is a travel finance strategist, writer, podcaster, speaker and the founder of Thought-Card.com. The Thought Card is an award-winning affordable travel finance blog and podcast about affording travel, paying off debt and building wealth. Danielle has traveled to over 26 countries and she refuses to let her financial responsibilities hold her back from pursuing her dreams. Iceland continues to be one of Danielle's favorite countries and she tries to visit at least once a year.

@thedanielledesir
www.thoughtcard.com

www.travelingblackwomen.com

www.ingramcontent.com/pod-product-compliance
Lightning Source LLC
Chambersburg PA
CBHW040855120626
46551CB00001B/33